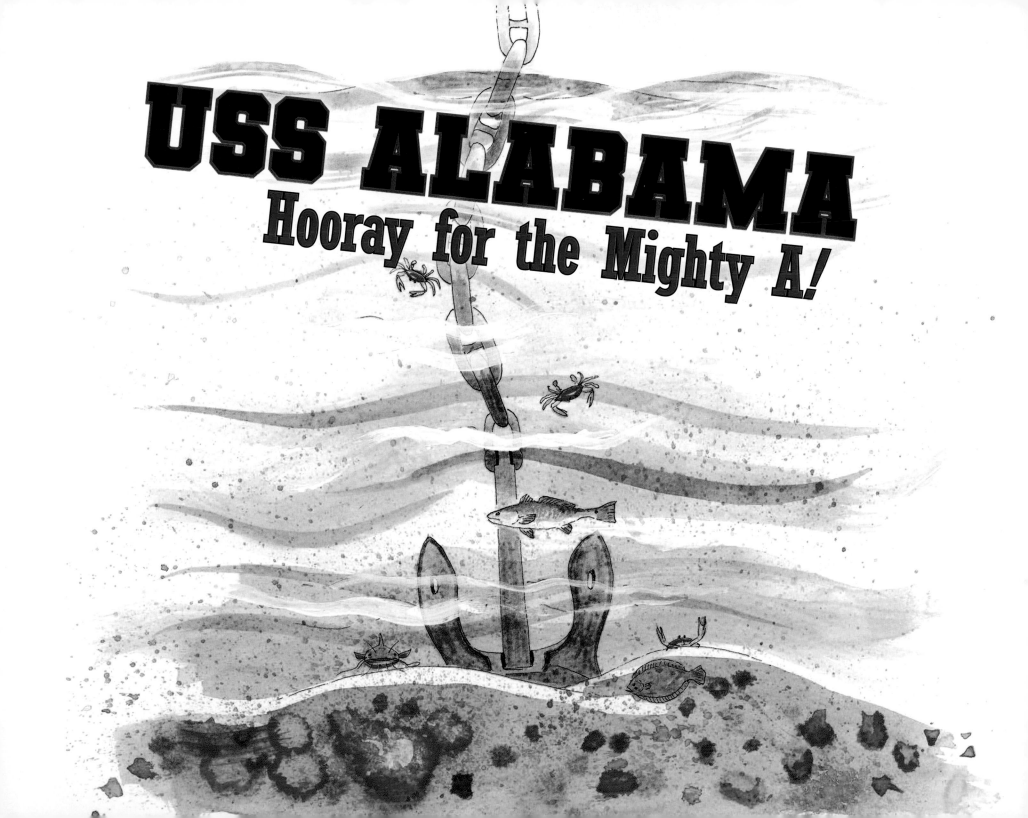

USS ALABAMA
Hooray for the Mighty A!

By Karyn W. Tunks

Illustrated by Julie Dupré Buckner

PELICAN PUBLISHING

NEW ORLEANS

This book is dedicated to the men and women of the United States military, the Alabama schoolchildren and citizens who contributed to the 1964 "Save the Battleship" fundraising campaign, and the many visitors who walk the decks of the USS Alabama
—KT and JDB

First River Road Press edition, 2015
First Pelican edition, 2023

The word "Pelican" and the depiction of a pelican are trademarks of Arcadia Publishing Company Inc. and are registered in the U.S. Patent and Trademark Office.

Our heartfelt thanks to Bill Tunnell, executive director; Shea McLean, curator; and all the other excellent staff at the USS *Alabama* Battleship Memorial Park for their support and guidance on this project.

100,000 thanks to Linda Kay Loper (childhood "Save the Battleship" contributor) for sharing this great story of how Alabama's children saved the Mighty A.

Photograph page 32, top, courtesy of USS ALABAMA Battleship Commission.
Photograph page 32, bottom, courtesy of Cynthia Tunnell.

ISBN 9781455627769

Printed in Korea
Published by Pelican Publishing
New Orleans, LA
www.pelicanpub.com

BOOM! BOOM! BOOM!
The big guns on the **deck** of the mighty battleship fired into the night.

BOOM!
    BOOM!
        BOOM!
The blasts were so strong they lit
up the sky like the 4th of July.

BOOM! BOOM! BOOM! **Heavy artillery** reached
its target twenty miles across the ocean.

The USS *Alabama* successfully completed her mission!

The guns came to rest, but there was still work for the **crew** to do. From the **bridge** the **captain**'s voice rang out, "Now hear this . . . Now hear this . . . " and he ordered the sailors to prepare to get **underway**.

Ship propellers as big as trucks began to churn below the water's surface and the great battleship charted a new **course**.

ATLANTIC

PACIFIC

The final battle of the USS *Alabama* took place on 17 July 1945. During World War II (WWII), the fine battleship steamed across the Atlantic and Pacific Oceans earning nine **battle stars**. The ship kept her crew safe during many battles and never suffered significant damage because of enemy fire. Sailors and Marines called her the "Mighty A."

For more than three years, 2,500 men called the USS *Alabama* home. She was a floating city where sailors worked, slept, ate, and played. Bunks were stacked five high to give every man a place to sleep. The ship was so big she housed a barber shop, a dentist's office, and even a jail cell.

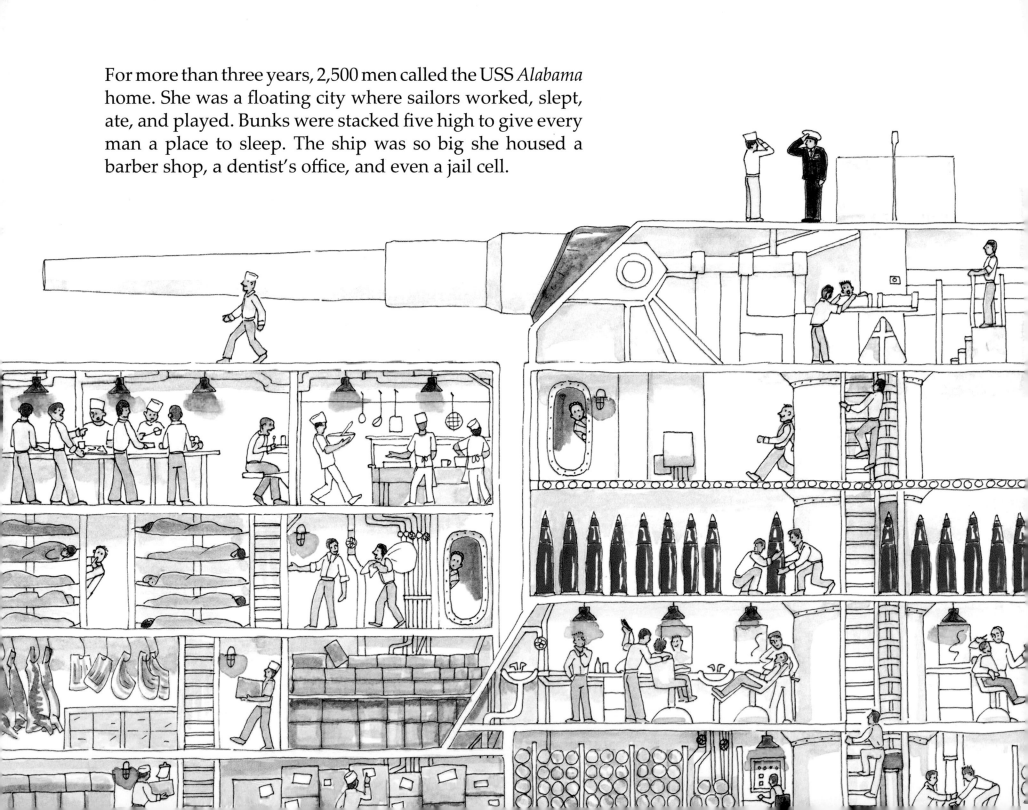

Every morning the cooks in the **galley** made 320 gallons of coffee and baked 550 loaves of bread.

For a treat, the men visited the **"gedunk stand"** for candy, a cold soda, or a scoop of freshly made ice cream.

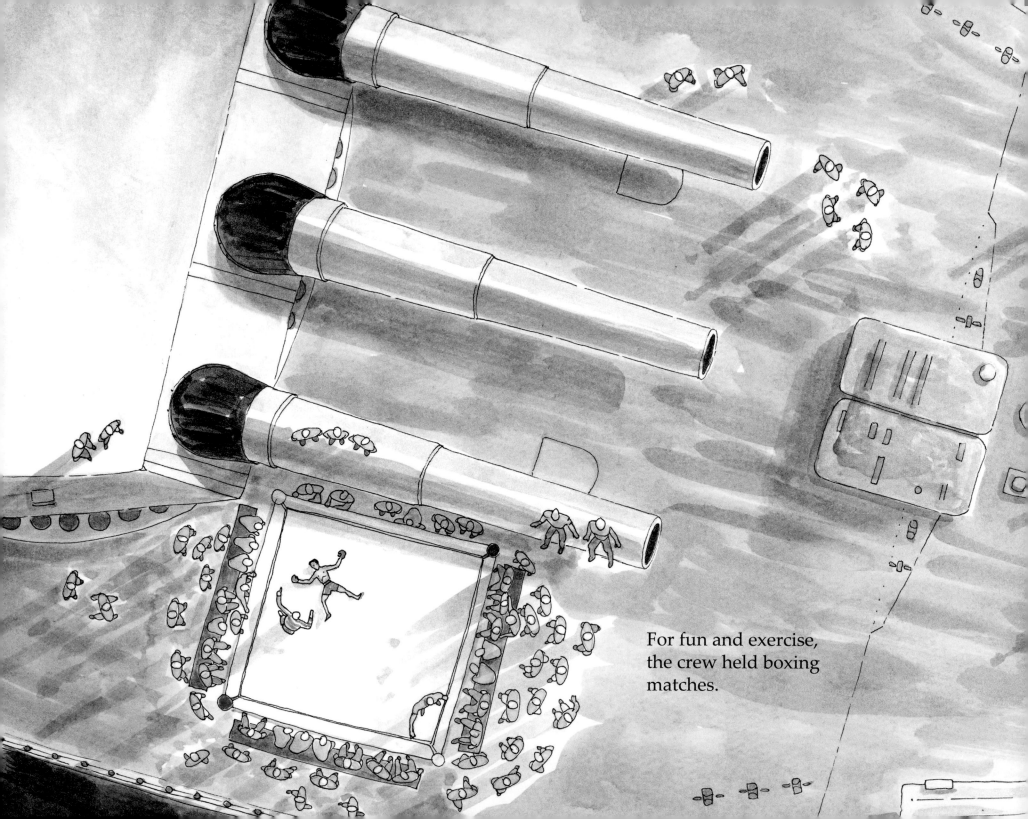

For fun and exercise,
the crew held boxing
matches.

Volleyball was played on deck using any object that the sailors could hit that would not bounce overboard!

In the ship's library, sailors checked out books to read and received mail from home. At night, movies were shown on deck or the ship's band entertained the crew.

The sailors on the Mighty A worked hard, but they had a lot of fun, too.

After WWII ended in 1945, many battleships were no longer needed. The once-powerful vessels were towed to the Navy Yard, where they sat empty and silent.

Some of the ships were sold for salvage, then chopped up, melted down, and used to make household items like razor blades.

The USS *Alabama* sat in the Washington State Navy Yard for fifteen years awaiting her fate. Then officials decided that the battleship had finished her work defending our country. In 1962, officials gave the order to dismantle and scrap the Mighty A.

The people of Alabama did not want
the majestic battleship that had been named for their
state to be destroyed. They made plans to collect money
and buy the ship. To raise enough money, all of the citizens
had to do their part, even the children!

FEED CAT 10¢
RAKE 20¢
WEED GARDEN 35¢
BABYSIT 30¢

CHUCK 55¢
JOAN 45¢
JANE 40¢

When they heard about the USS *Alabama*, schoolchildren wanted to help and joined the effort to "Save the Battleship." All across the state, from Huntsville to Mobile and every town in between, children brought pennies, nickels, dimes, and quarters to school. They worked to make money to rescue the battleship.

You Can Help Sail USS Alabama Home.

CHUCK

Joan

Jane

Children gave up
treats and donated their
allowance to preserve the battleship.
Instead of buying ice cream at school, they
donated their snack money to the effort. Some boys and girls did
extra chores to raise money. Others collected empty cola bottles
and returned them to stores for the two-cent deposit.

Their sacrifice and hard work paid off. In just one year, schoolchildren contributed almost $100,000. The money they earned and donated helped bring the USS *Alabama* home! The next challenge was moving the mighty ship.

For her final voyage, the USS *Alabama* was towed from the Navy Yard to the Panama Canal. There, she squeezed through the **locks** with only eleven inches to spare on each side. After a three-month voyage, the battleship appeared in Mobile Bay. On 14 September 1964, she arrived to a hero's welcome as people stood along the shoreline cheering, "Hooray for the Mighty A!"

Once the USS *Alabama* was safely **berthed** in Mobile Bay, the schoolchildren were invited to visit. Because they helped save the ship, the children were given passes for free admission. They dashed from **bow** to **stern** and eagerly explored the ship's decks. The USS *Alabama* Battleship Memorial Park opened to all visitors on 9 January 1965.

Today, the USS *Alabama* is the most visible symbol of her namesake state. More than 15 million visitors from around the world have stood on her decks. Thousands of Boy Scouts and Girls Scouts have spent a night on board. Military veterans gather on the ship for reunions.

Hooray for the Mighty A!

Everyone feels honored to be in the presence of the great ship. But perhaps the proudest visitors of all are the schoolchildren who made it possible to bring the USS *Alabama* home. Today they bring their own children and even their grandchildren to visit the battleship and share the story of how they saved the Mighty A!

U.S.S. ALABAMA
CHARTER MEMBER

(NAME)

COMMISSION CHAIRMAN

GOVERNOR

Good For FREE Admission

GLOSSARY

Battle stars—Stars awarded to and often painted on the side of a ship for specific combat engagements.

Berthed—Having brought a ship to a space where it can dock or anchor.

Bow—Forward part of a ship.

Bridge—Place on a vessel where the crew steers a ship and controls its speed.

Captain—Person in command of a ship.

Course—Direction in which a ship is steered.

Crew—Team of people who work closely together to operate a ship.

Deck—Floor-like surface covering the hull, or main body, of a ship.

HATCH HATCH HATCH HATCH

SAND LOCKER

CREW'S WASHROOM ←—CREW'S BERTHING→ BAND ROOM CREW'S BERTHING

VOID

BOSUN'S STORAGE CREW'S WASHROOM CREW'S BERTHING CREW'S BERTHING E

UPPER SHELL HANDLI

PEAK TANK GEAR CREW'S BERTHING MESS ATTENDANTS BARBE SHOP

PAINT STORAGE ←—STORAGE→ ←—STORAGE—→ WINDLASS ROOM STORAGE CHAIN LOCKER

INFLAMMABLE LIQUIDS STORAGE PROVISIONS

←—PUMP ROOM—→

VOID FUEL OIL

Galley—Kitchen of the ship.

Gedunk stand—Place on a ship where ice cream, candy, and other snack foods are sold.

Heavy artillery—Mounted projectile-firing guns or missile launchers.

Locks—Short, confined sections of a waterway in which the water level can be changed to raise or lower ships.

Stern—The back of the ship.

Underway—Vessel in motion.

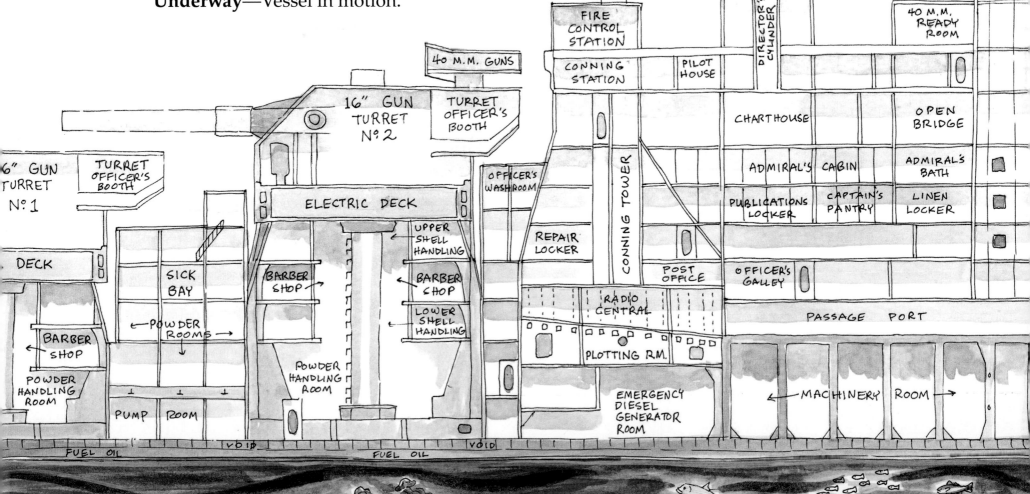

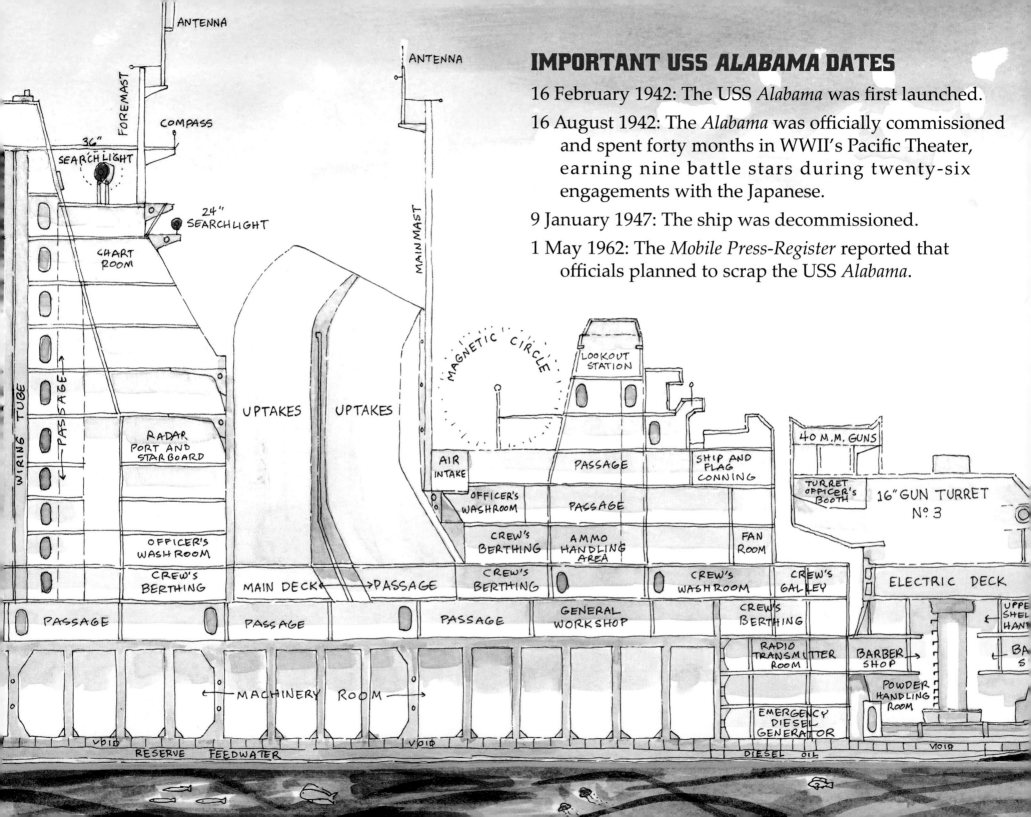

IMPORTANT USS *ALABAMA* DATES

16 February 1942: The USS *Alabama* was first launched.

16 August 1942: The *Alabama* was officially commissioned and spent forty months in WWII's Pacific Theater, earning nine battle stars during twenty-six engagements with the Japanese.

9 January 1947: The ship was decommissioned.

1 May 1962: The *Mobile Press-Register* reported that officials planned to scrap the USS *Alabama*.

12 September 1963: The USS *Alabama* Battleship Commission formed to save the ship.

11 June 1964: The ship was awarded to the state of Alabama.

14 September 1964: The ship entered Mobile Bay after a three-month tow.

9 January 1965: USS *Alabama* Battleship Memorial Park opened.

14 January 1986: The ship was declared a National Historic Landmark.

9 January 2015: The USS *Alabama* Battleship Memorial Park celebrated its 50th anniversary.

SCHOOLBUS: 35' LONG

HUMPBACK WHALE: 48' LONG

BLUE WHALE: 98' LONG

USS ALABAMA: 608.8' LONG

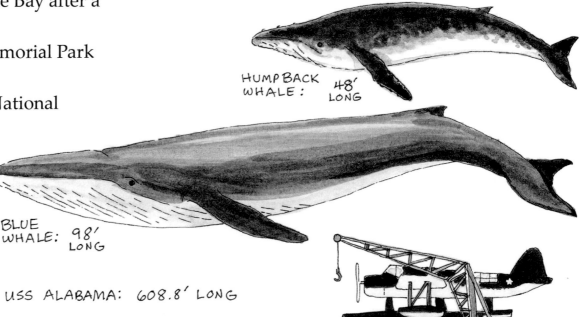

AIRPLANE CRANE

VENT   HATCH   HATCH

SCULLERY | JAIL | CREW'S MESSING SPACE   CREW'S MESSING SPACE | PANTRY | MESSROOM | AIRPLANE CRANE

PASSAGE | CREW'S BERTHING   CREW'S BERTHING | LAUNDRY RECEIVING | LAUNDRY | MACHINERY

REFRIGERATOR ROOM | THAW ROOM | ICE AND REFRIGERATOR RM.   MORE GEAR   STEERING GEAR   GASOLINE

PROVISIONS | PROVISIONS   VOID

A Message from the Director.

A short five decades ago, in the spring of 1964, about one million Alabama schoolchildren had no idea that Battleship USS *Alabama* (BB-60) even existed, much less that she was about to come to the great State of Alabama with their help.

When the statewide campaign was announced to bring the battleship back 'home,' there was a sense of surprise and amazement. Really? A battleship named *Alabama*? Coming to Mobile? And we can help? Wow! This is big!

As a senior in high school that year, I shared the amazement with my classmates and school. All around Alabama, school kids like me began saving pennies, nickels, dimes, whatever, from milk and lunch money to make the impossible dream happen.

And happen it did. Those schoolchildren collected almost $100,000 that spring at a time when the minimum wage was $1.00 and you could buy a Cadillac for about $3,000. Almost one million dollars was raised statewide by Alabama citizens and the USS *Alabama* Battleship Memorial Park opened to the public on Saturday, January 9, 1965.

Today the park and her National Historic Landmark Battleship USS *Alabama* stands as the most visible and recognizable symbol of our state and perhaps the most unique military attraction in all these United States. More than 15 million visitors from all over the world have toured the park.

The most important fact is that schoolchildren and other Alabamians made the dream happen. Today the USS *Alabama* Battleship Commission salutes this remarkable book that tells the story of that amazing time in Alabama history. No book has told the story so accurately!

It's with a great sense of pride that not only do I want you to read this, but come see us!

Very Respectfully,

Bill Tunnell,
executive director
USS *Alabama* Battleship Memorial Park